D1557947

SHARKS SET I

WHALE SHARKS

Heidi Mathea
ABDO Publishing Company

visit us at
www.abdopublishing.com

Published by ABDO Publishing Company, 8000 West 78th Street, Edina, Minnesota 55439. Copyright © 2011 by Abdo Consulting Group, Inc. International copyrights reserved in all countries. No part of this book may be reproduced in any form without written permission from the publisher. The Checkerboard Library™ is a trademark and logo of ABDO Publishing Company.

Printed in the United States of America, North Mankato, Minnesota.
042010
092010

 PRINTED ON RECYCLED PAPER

Cover Photo: © James D. Watt/SeaPics.com
Interior Photos: Alamy pp. 11, 12–13; © Amar & Isabelle Guillen/SeaPics.com p. 15;
    © James D. Watt/SeaPics.com pp. 5, 17; Peter Arnold pp. 6, 8, 18–19, 21;
    Uko Gorter pp. 7, 9

Editor: BreAnn Rumsch
Art Direction & Cover Design: Neil Klinepier

Library of Congress Cataloging-in-Publication Data

Mathea, Heidi, 1979-
  Whale sharks / Heidi Mathea.
      p. cm. -- (Sharks)
  Includes index.
  ISBN 978-1-61613-430-3
  1. Whale shark--Juvenile literature. I. Title.

  QL638.95.R4M38 2011
  597.3--dc22
                                    2010007288

CONTENTS

Whale Sharks and Family

Sharks are fascinating creatures. Today, there are more than 400 shark species swimming worldwide.

All sharks share similar features. They do not have bones. Instead, their skeletons are made of a tough, stretchy material called cartilage. Grab your nose and wiggle it back and forth. That's cartilage!

Tiny, toothlike scales called denticles cover shark skin. Denticles offer protection for the skin. And, they allow sharks to move more easily through water. This rough covering is **unique** to sharks.

Sharks come in all shapes and sizes. The whale shark is the biggest shark species and the world's

largest fish. This slow-moving giant is one of three
large filter-feeder sharks. These sharks use their
gills to strain food from ocean water.

Whale sharks are the only members of the family Rhincodontidae.

WHAT THEY LOOK LIKE

Whale sharks are huge fish. They are capable of growing nearly 60 feet (18 m) long. That's awesome! Most whale sharks are 39 feet (12 m) long and weigh about 15 tons (14 t).

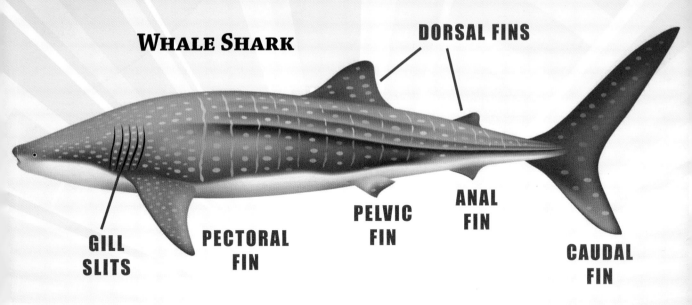

WHALE SHARK

DORSAL FINS

GILL SLITS

PECTORAL FIN

PELVIC FIN

ANAL FIN

CAUDAL FIN

The whale shark has a wide, flattened head and large gill slits. Its mouth is nearly at the end of its snout. More than 600 rows of tiny teeth fill this huge mouth. Yet, this shark does not use its teeth for feeding.

This long, thick shark displays a **unique** color pattern. Its back is grayish, bluish, or brownish. Light spots and stripes form a checkerboard pattern on this dark background. The whale shark's belly is white.

The whale shark's fins keep this large shark stable and allow it to steer. The large caudal fin, or tail, moves the shark through the water.

WHERE THEY LIVE

Whale sharks like warm ocean water. They live in almost all **tropical** and warm **temperate** seas. But, they do not occupy the Mediterranean Sea.

Whale sharks live throughout the Indian Ocean. In the Atlantic Ocean, these sharks range from New York to central Brazil. And, they are found from Senegal in Africa to the Gulf of Guinea.

In the Pacific Ocean, whale sharks range from Japan to

Researchers believe whale sharks migrate seasonally.

Where Do Whale Sharks Live?

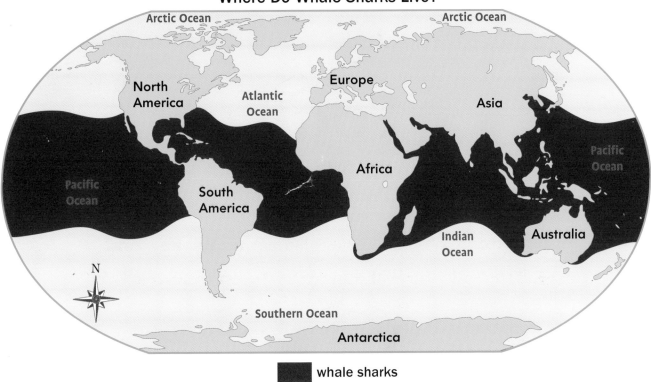

whale sharks

Australia. They also live off Hawaii's coasts and from California to Chile.

These gentle giants swim near the water's surface. They are often spotted far offshore. But they also travel inshore. Whale sharks are usually found alone. However, they have been seen in schools of more than 100 members.

FOOD

Whale sharks feed at or near the water's surface. As filter feeders, these giant sharks feast on a variety of **plankton**. Whale sharks also eat **mollusks**. And they feed on fish, such as sardines, mackerel, and tuna.

Sometimes the whale shark feeds in a vertical position, with its head pointed toward the surface. As the shark bobs up and down, food enters its mouth.

However, this shark usually feeds while cruising through the water. It opens its mouth and sucks in food and water. This action works much like a vacuum cleaner!

When its huge mouth is full, the whale shark closes its jaws. This traps prey and water inside. To get to its food, the shark forces the water out through

its gills. The gills act like strainers, filtering food from the water. The whale shark swallows anything retained in its mouth.

Whale sharks find lots of yummy food at the water's surface.

SENSES

As the largest fish in the world, whale sharks must find lots of food. Their sense of smell plays a large role in hunting. Their sense of taste is well developed, too.

Many sharks also use their eyes to find food. However, whale sharks have small eyes that are located far back on their heads. So, researchers do not believe eyesight helps whale sharks hunt.

All sharks use sense **organs** in their heads to detect electric fields. Every living animal constantly gives off its own weak electric field. Even if a shark cannot see its prey, it can detect this field.

Special sense organs run down each side of a shark's body. This lateral line system allows sharks to detect the vibrations of other animals in the water. This can lead the shark to its next meal or warn it of danger.

Sharks have been called "swimming noses" because of their excellent sense of smell.

BABIES

Researchers know little about whale shark reproduction. Most of their information is from a female whale shark captured in 1995. She was carrying 300 baby sharks inside her. The babies were 17 to 25 inches (42 to 63 cm) long.

This discovery told researchers that whale shark mothers do not lay their eggs. The eggs hatch inside the mother, and the babies continue to develop there. Eventually, the mother gives birth to live young.

Newborn whale sharks are called pups. Researchers believe the pups measure 21 to 25 inches (53 to 63.5 cm) long at birth. It is not yet known how many pups are born in a **litter**.

Whale shark pups are on their own once they are born. Luckily, they can swim and their senses are fully developed.

ATTACK AND DEFENSE

The whale shark is lucky to be so huge! It does not have to worry much about predators. Few animals would even attempt to take on this large creature.

However, these sharks are not so mammoth at birth. So, young whale sharks have a little more to fear than adults. They have been found in the stomachs of other shark species.

The whale shark's skin may play a role in its defense. It is up to six inches (15 cm) thick! Not much can easily cut through it. Yet, **parasites** may attach themselves to the shark's skin. Whale sharks often rub against boats to remove these unwelcome guests.

The whale shark's large mouth is perfectly suited to filter feeding. It is not made to grab large prey.

ATTACKS ON HUMANS

Whale sharks are little threat to humans. Sometimes, divers approach these gentle sharks and even ride them! Whale sharks are curious about people, too. They may swim nearby people to check them out.

Human interaction with these giants is not always gentle. Whale sharks have bumped into boats. And, boaters have run into these giant fish.

This is because whale sharks often swim near the water's surface. They spend their days cruising the ocean for their next meals. These immense fish are amazing sights to see!

WHALE SHARK FACTS

Scientific name:

Whale shark   *Rhincodon typus*

Average Size:

Whale sharks are about 39 feet (12 m) long and weigh 15 tons (14 t).

Where They're Found:

Whale sharks live all over the world in warm ocean waters.

GLOSSARY

litter - all of the pups born at one time to a mother shark.

mollusk - any of a group of animals with a soft body usually enclosed in a shell. Clams, snails, and squids are all mollusks.

organ - a part of an animal or a plant composed of several kinds of tissues. An organ performs a specific function. The heart, liver, gallbladder, and intestines are organs of an animal.

parasite - an organism that lives on or in another organism of a different species.

plankton - small animals and plants that float in a body of water.

temperate - relating to an area where average temperatures range between 50 and 55 degrees Fahrenheit (10 and 13°C).

tropical - relating to an area with an average temperature above 77 degrees Fahrenheit (25°C) where no freezing occurs.

unique - being the only one of its kind.

WEB SITES

To learn more about whale sharks, visit ABDO Publishing Company on the World Wide Web at **www.abdopublishing.com**. Web sites about whale sharks are featured on our Book Links page. These links are routinely monitored and updated to provide the most current information available.

INDEX